JIM BURNS AND MIKE DEVRIES

Gospel Light

PUBLISHING STAFF

William T. Greig, Chairman

Kyle Duncan, Publisher

Dr. Elmer L. Towns, Senior Consulting Publisher

Pam Weston, Senior Editor

Patti Pennington Virtue, Associate Editor

Jeff Kempton, Editorial Assistant

Hilary Young, Editorial Assistant

Bayard Taylor, M.Div., Senior Editor, Biblical and Theological Issues

Kevin Parks, Cover Designer

Roseanne Richardson, Cover Production

Debi Thayer/Zelle Olson, Designers

ISBN 0-8307-2921-6
© 2002 Gospel Light
All rights reserved.
Printed in the U.S.A.

How to Make Clean Copies from This Book

Contents

Object Lessons

Case Studies

Discussion Starters

Indexes

Dedication

We dedicate this book to our fearless leader and COO at YouthBuilders: Todd Dean. Thank you for making projects like this one a reality and for taking your incredible abilities and talents and using them for God! We appreciate you.

—Jim Burns and Mike DeVries

Acknowledgments

Special thanks to:

Jim Liebelt—Jim's writing, editing and focusing skills helped greatly with this book. Not only is Jim an excellent writer and talented editor, but he is also a wonderful friend.

Carrie Steele—As assistant to Jim Burns, Carrie has time and again gone far beyond the call of duty to help edit, organize and keep Jim on track. She is one of the most talented people we know and is a joy to work with in ministry.

Mark Simone—Mark is one of the most creative people on planet Earth. What more can be said?!

Jean Tippit—Jean's contributions to this project proved once again that she is a joy to work with and continues to be a creative and wonderful voice in the youth-ministry world.

Contributors

Mike DeVries
Vice President of Family-Based Youth Ministry, YouthBuilders
San Juan Capistrano, California
16-year youth-ministry veteran

Jim Liebelt
Director, YouthBuilders New England
Hull, Massachusetts
19-year youth-ministry veteran

Mark Simone
Associate Minister with Youth
Chagrin Falls, Ohio
Writer and leader of youth-ministry training events all over the world
22-year youth-ministry veteran

Jean Tippit
Speaker, Writer and Youth Ministry Volunteer
Mobile, Alabama
17-year youth-ministry veteran

Introduction

Every Tuesday night for the past couple of years our local public high school has had its Fellowship of Christian Athletes (FCA) meeting in our home. My role is simply as Christy, Rebecca and Heidi's dad—the guy who provides lots of food. The group has only asked me to be a guest speaker one time. One of the guys came up to me afterward and said, "Mr. Burns, you should really think about doing this for a living!"

As a weekly observer I've noticed that the best meetings with the most energy are always the meetings with interaction and discussion. Participation seems to be the ingredient for a successful youth meeting. When someone talks *at* the students, the success of the meeting is dependent on the speaker being dynamic or on the subject hitting the mark. When there is group interaction and discussion, however, the meeting works almost every time.

Over the years it's been noted that students learn best when *they* talk, not when *you* talk. Sure, we must learn to communicate and in many situations we have to give a message, but by far the best learning experiences happen through group discussion and interaction. That's where books like this one can be so helpful. Mike DeVries and I love to speak, but we have found a better way to develop effective long-term learning experiences: using creative object lessons, case studies and discussion starters.

The good news is that you do not need to be a gifted speaker to affect the learning and spiritual growth of your students. More important is becoming a good facilitator of communication and interaction. This is a resource book to help you do just that.

Thank you for your involvement in the lives of kids and their families. You are making an eternal difference.

Jim Burns, Ph.D.
President, YouthBuilders

Object Lessons

Any Light Makes a Difference

The Big Idea

Discover the impact that light has on darkness and how Christians are to serve as light in a dark world.

Materials Needed

- ❑ A small flashlight
- ❑ A large battery powered lantern
- ❑ A small penlight or candle for each person
- ❑ A few lighters (if you use the candles)
- ❑ A box large enough to cover the lantern
- ❑ A dark meeting room

Preparation

Make the room as dark as possible. Assemble all of the materials.

Turn out the lights in the room and begin speaking in the darkness. Explain: **In Matthew 5:14-16, Jesus taught that Christians are like lights set on a hill and that the light would be no good if it were hidden.** Use the different lights to illustrate the following points about light and Christians as lights in a dark world:

- One small flashlight: **Even a small light in darkness will make a difference. There is no Christian who is less important or has less to do. All light, no matter what the size, will shatter the darkness.**
- The large lantern and the box: **This large lantern will drastically change the darkness. But if you put a box or blanket over it, it cannot be seen. If we hide our light, it will have no effect on the dark world.**
- Hand out the penlights (or candles), instructing students not to turn them on yet. Turn out all other lights; then light one penlight (or lighter, and have adult leaders walk around and light the candles one at a time). Explain how one light lighting another light brightens the world.

Discussion Questions

1. How do Christians hide Christ's light?

2. Give an example of a Christian that you know who shines, giving light to everyone around.

3. How can you be a light in the darkness on your school campus during the next week?

Possible Topics

Making a difference; Christians as Christ's light in the world

Scripture Passages

Matthew 5:14-16; John 1:3-5; 3:19-21; 8:12; 12:46; Acts 13:47; Romans 13:12; 2 Corinthians 4:6; 6:12; Ephesians 5:8-14; 1 John 2:9-11

The Apple Cart

The Big Idea

Just as apples come in a wide variety of colors, shapes and sizes and serve different purposes, so do human beings. God has made each of us unique and with different purposes in mind.

Materials Needed

❑ A plastic toy wheelbarrow

❑ Several each of the following varieties of apples: Granny Smith, Red Delicious and Fuji

Preparation

Layer the apples in the wheelbarrow, making sure to keep each with its own kind.

As the meeting begins, point out the wheelbarrow. Point out the three very different types of apples and highlight the differences not only in color, but also in taste, texture, uses (e.g., some are better suited for baking) and region in which they are grown. Pick up one of each of the varieties and explain: **As unique as each variety may be, every one of these is still an apple.** Discuss: **How are people similar to these apples?** Allow for responses; then continue: **We are all unique; each one of us has something that's different from anyone else in the world. When someone uses these differences as an excuse to dislike—and sometimes even hate—others, it's called prejudice. Prejudice is judging others based on what can be seen with our eyes and not bothering to find out who they really are inside.**

Ask volunteers to share about their own experience or the experience of someone they know who's been the target of prejudice. Allow for several responses; then ask a volunteer to read Romans 10:12 and discuss: **What does this verse tell us about God's view of prejudice? Why do we make distinctions between ourselves and others?**

Possible Topics

Prejudice, racism, diversity, the unity of the Body of Christ

Scripture Passages

Romans 10:12; Galatians 3:26-29; Colossians 3:11-17

Commitment Is Costly

The Big Idea

Commitment to Christ comes with a cost: your life.

Materials Needed

❑ An egg

❑ A piece of ham or bacon

Hold the egg in one hand and the ham (or bacon) in the other. Discuss: **Which animal displayed more commitment in providing this food: the chicken or the pig? Why?**

Continue: **Clearly, the pig had to commit more than the chicken—it cost the pig its life to provide us with ham (bacon). Real commitment to Christ is also costly. Total commitment means we give up ownership of our lives to Him.** Share the following verse; then discuss the questions:

> Then he said to them all: "If anyone would come after me, he must deny himself and take up his cross daily and follow me. For whoever wants to save his life will lose it, but whoever loses his life for me will save it. What good is it for a man to gain the whole world, and yet lose or forfeit his very self?" (Luke 9:23-25).

Discussion Questions

1. Which of your behaviors and actions reflect the Lord's ownership of your life?

2. Name something you would not be willing to do for Jesus.

3. If you were in a situation that you knew would result in losing your life if you admitted that you were a Christian, what would you do? Why?

Possible Topics

Self-denial; following Christ; the cost of discipleship

Scripture Passages

1 Chronicles 21:24; Luke 14:25-35; Romans 12:1-2; Philippians 3:7-10

Dealing with Past Sins

The Big Idea

Jesus' death on the cross and His resurrection from the dead have the power to cleanse us from all of our sins: past, present and future. His forgiveness is available to each of us, simply for the asking.

Materials Needed

❑ Clear drinking glass

❑ Water

❑ Blue food coloring

❑ Liquid bleach

Preparation

Fill the glass about two-thirds full with water.

Explain how sin darkens our lives. As you talk, list specific sins and place a drop of blue food coloring in the glass of water for each sin you list. Be careful not to use too many drops of food coloring. Next discuss how Jesus died and was resurrected to cleanse us and remove all of our sins, guilt and shame. As you speak about what Jesus has done for us, pour some liquid bleach (take care not to splash it onto your clothing or carpet) into the tinted water. The bleach will dissolve the food color and return the water to clear—though some yellowish tint may remain. **Note:** While red food coloring would work better symbolically, blue food coloring dissolves better than red in this object lesson. Share the following verse:

> "**Come now, let us reason together,**" says the LORD. "**Though your sins are like scarlet, they shall be as white as snow; though they are red as crimson, they shall be like wool**" **(Isaiah 1:18).**

The sins of our past can make it difficult to experience the freedom that God desires for us to have in the present and in the future. The blood of Christ that cleanses us from all sin is like the bleach in the colored water. When we come to God and humbly confess our sins and ask Him to forgive us and give us a clean slate, He grants our request! Our sinful past is immediately cleansed and wiped away forever!

Discussion Questions

1. How does it make you feel to know that God is willing and able to forgive any and all of your past sins?

2. What difference should it make in how we live our lives, knowing that God forgives our sins? What did it cost God to provide salvation and redeem us from our sins?

3. Why do so many people refuse to come to God to confess their sins and ask for His forgiveness?

4. How does your life reflect thanks to God for His forgiveness?

Possible Topics

Dealing with your past; sin; God's love; God's forgiveness

Scripture Passages

Psalm 51; Isaiah 1:18; John 10:10; Galatians 5:1; Hebrews 9:14; 10:19-22; 1 John 1:9

Don't Fall!

The Big Idea

Without faith *and* works, our Christian lives don't go anywhere.

Materials Needed

❑ A scooter

Display the scooter. Ask for a volunteer to demonstrate how the scooter works (or demonstrate it yourself). Discuss what it takes to ride a scooter successfully. Make the point that it takes two important things to be able to ride a scooter: balance and the ability to use one foot to propel the scooter. Without balance, you would fall off. Without using your foot to propel yourself, you wouldn't go anywhere even if you maintained your balance. Read the following:

> **Faith by itself, if it is not accompanied by action, is dead. But someone will say, "You have faith; I have deeds." Show me your faith without deeds, and I will show you my faith by what I do (James 2:17-18).**

Explain: **Riding a scooter can be compared to being a growing, useful Christian. You need two important things to make the Christian life work: faith and works. Without faith, works may be helpful to other people, but they don't make you a Christian. Without works, faith is sterile. There would be little or no growth in your life, and you would not be a witness to others for Christ. Faith and works together will cause your Christian life to grow in leaps and bounds. You'll go places for God!** You could ride off on the scooter to demonstrate the point!

Discussion Questions

1. What does "faith by itself . . . is dead" mean?

2. What makes works without faith just as dead as faith without works?

3. Describe a time when you have tried to do works in your own power without relying on God—faith. What happened?

4. If you were arrested for the charge of being a Christian, would there be enough evidence to convict you?

Possible Topics

Christian life; faith and works; Christian growth

Scripture Passages

Galatians 5:6; 1 Thessalonians 1:3; James 2:14-26; Revelation 2:19

Exposed!

The Big Idea

Having sex before marriage is like exposing the film in your camera to light and ruining the pictures you have taken.

Materials Needed

❑ A camera
❑ A roll of film

Take several pictures of the group. Try to get everyone involved in the fun. Make sure you take a lot and that everyone is in one or two pictures. (**Caution:** If you have a camera that will automatically rewind at the end of the roll, be sure to stop short of the last picture or your object lesson will be lost!) Have fun getting some of the following:

- A picture of each grade
- Pictures of several groups of friends
- A picture of the youngest and the oldest together
- A picture of the shortest and the tallest together
- A whole group picture
- Some silly pictures

After taking the pictures, talk about what you plan to do with the pictures. You could say that you will give them to the students, make a bulletin board, use them as gifts for their parents or post them on your website. Talk about how much fun it is to look at photos when you pick them up from the developers. If possible, have students talk about what they like about photos.

After a brief discussion, stop and exclaim: **I want to see these pictures now. I just can't wait!** Open the camera and expose the film. Work fast because some may try to stop you. There may be booing, hissing, moaning and groaning.

After everyone settles down, discuss how exposing this film too soon is like having premarital sex. Sex was designed to be saved for marriage and is a good thing in the right place, but outside of marriage it is like exposing the film too soon.

Discussion Questions

1. Why do you think God designed sexual intercourse to be expressed only within the context of marriage?

2. What are the dangers of having sex before marriage?

3. What are the benefits of maintaining sexual purity before marriage?

4. What can you do to avoid falling into sexual temptation?

Possible Topics

Sexual purity; God's design for sexuality; living according to God's will

Scripture Passages

Genesis 2:20b-25; Exodus 20:14; 1 Corinthians 6:13-20; Ephesians 5:1-3; 1 Thessalonians 4:3-6

First Things First!

The Big Idea

When we put God first, everything else in life falls into its proper place.

Materials Needed

- ❑ A table
- ❑ A large, empty, plastic mayonnaise or peanut butter jar with the labels removed
- ❑ Walnuts in the shells
- ❑ Gravel and sand

> **Note:** As an option you could use a one-gallon jar and fist-sized rocks instead of the plastic jar and walnuts.

Preparation

Measure out the exact amount of walnuts, gravel and sand needed to fill the jar to the top. Ideally, everything should fit if you put in the walnuts first, then the gravel, then the sand and finally put the lid on.

Explain that this jar represents a normal day in our lives. Start by placing all the sand in the jar. As you pour, say that the sand represents activities such as talking on the phone, sports, music, TV, Internet, video games, etc. Next pour in the gravel, and explain that it represents school, homework, eating, sleeping, spending time with family, etc. Finally, try to cram in as many walnuts as possible with each one representing an aspect of our daily walk with Christ. One walnut could represent prayer, another Scripture reading, another witnessing, another fellowship with Christians, etc. Of course, only a few walnuts will fit, and you will barely be able to put the lid on the jar. When the jar is nice and full, still lacking most of the walnuts, you can pass it around, pointing out how stressed the jar is, nearly to the point of cracking.

Explain: **It is important to decide what to put first in your lives. If we start by putting the less important things in our lives ahead of spending time with God, not only will we run out of room for Him, but we will be so busy that we stress out and start failing at our other daily activities.**

Empty the jar and reverse the order. First place all of the walnuts into the jar, explaining the role of each one in our lives with God. Next pour in all of the gravel, talking about the importance of school, homework, time with family, eating and sleeping. Finally, pour the sand into the jar, discussing hang time with friends, sports, music, TV, video games, etc. If you measured correctly and practiced a time or two, all of the ingredients will fit and the lid can be closed without cracking or stressing the jar. Conclude the object lesson by reading the following verse:

Seek first his kingdom and his righteousness, and all these things will be given to you as well (Matthew 6:33).

Explain: **Our lives are filled with people, activities and issues that grab our attention, many of which are good and/or important things, but some aren't so good for us and are even a waste of our time. It is extremely important that we give our time to the people, activities and issues that are the most important. In our own priorities, our lives should reflect that we put God first.** Pick up a few of the walnuts. **These walnuts represented our time with God. If we don't put God first, often He will be crowded out by everything else we do and there will end up being no room for Him in our lives. If we put God first, He promises that everything else of importance will fall into place. A very godly man named Martin Luther once spoke of the importance of spending time with God among all of the other things we do each day. He said, "I have so much to do that I spend several hours in prayer before I am able to do it."**[1] **If you want to get everything done in your life that needs to be done, remember to put your relationship with God first; He will take care of the rest.**

Discussion Questions

1. What happens when we make our relationship with God our first priority?

2. Give an example of a time when you have put other things first in your life before God. What was the result?

3. How would your life change if you always put God first?

Possible Topics

Priorities in life; putting God first; time management

Scripture Passages

Psalm 23:1; 37:4; Proverbs 3:6; Matthew 6:33; Philippians 4:19

Note
1. Mark Water, compiler, *The New Encyclopedia of Christian Quotations*, (Grand Rapids, MI: Baker Books, 2000), p. 764.

The Flush

The Big Idea

God's forgiveness flushes our sin away.

Materials Needed

- ❑ An old toilet
- ❑ Concrete blocks or bricks
- ❑ Lots of water—both dirty water and clean
- ❑ A child-sized plastic swimming pool
- ❑ A white board, chalkboard or flip chart and pens or chalk
- ❑ Optional: Small slips of paper and pens or pencils

Preparation

Used toilets can be found at remodeling projects, building-supply recycling places or even a junkyard—the dirtier and more beat up the better.

Set up the toilet securely on the concrete blocks or bricks in the plastic swimming pool. Fill the toilet bowl with scummy water—either add dirt/garbage to the water or make the church custodian ecstatic and offer to wash the floor at the church (you may want to have smelling salts in case he or she faints from shock!). Then, after letting the water sit for a day or two—the smellier the better—pour the gray water into the bowl. Fill the *tank* with clean water. **Note:** This lesson is best done outside, but just remember that if you choose to do it inside, you will eventually need to get the water out of the meeting room!

As you discuss sin, have students list the sins they see being committed all around them every day. You might want to bring in examples found in news articles, song lyrics and/or movie and TV themes to get the sharing started. Write down their responses on the board or flip chart. Guide students to respond with specific examples of everyday sins.

Liken sin to the dirty water in the toilet bowl. Explain: **It's smelly and contaminated. There is nothing we can do on our own to clean the water, and there is nothing we can put in the water to clean it up. We can try to hide the smell by using air fresheners that cover up the smell for a short time but not permanently. We can pour disinfectant in it, but that doesn't get rid of the dirt and the contamination will return. Just as with our own sin, we need help in cleaning up the mess.**

As we confess our sin to God, He cleanses us. He flushes out all the filth in our lives, and we are clean. At this point flush the toilet. The dirty water will be flushed out, and the bowl will be filled with clean water.

Option: Give each student a slip of paper and a pen or pencil. Instruct them to write the sins with which they struggle on the papers and then throw the papers in the toilet—***prior to flushing***. Use this as a visual image to personalize their confession and cleansing in God's eyes.

Discussion Questions

1. In what ways does sin harm us? Why?

2. How does our sin affect other people?

3. What is the difference between being sorry for your sin and true repentance?

4. Does confession mean we can sin and still be pals with God? Or does God hope for something else from our confession?

Possible Topics

Sin and God's forgiveness; Christian life

Scripture Passages

Romans 3:22-24; 6:23; 12:1-2; Galatians 5:16-21; Ephesians 4:22-31; 5:3-8; Hebrews 3:13; 1 John 1:6-9; 2:1-6,15-17

Follow the Instructions

The Big Idea

The Bible is God's instruction manual for living life the way He intended.

Materials Needed

❑ A small, unassembled item (an appliance, model, etc.) with a lot of parts *and* an instructional manual

Display the unassembled item, showing the large number of parts. Discuss: **There are two options for assembling this item: (1) you can ignore the instruction manual, begin assembling the parts and hope for the best, or (2) you can use the instruction manual and follow its guidance for assembling the item. Option:** If you have time, have two groups try to assemble identical items, but give only one group the instructions. Share the following:

> **All Scripture is God-breathed and is useful for teaching, rebuking, correcting and training in righteousness, so that the man of God may be thoroughly equipped for every good work (2 Timothy 3:16-17).**

Explain: **Some people choose to assemble items without consulting the instruction manual. Sometimes it works out and the item turns out okay, functioning as it was intended to work. Yet many times, as a direct result of ignoring the instruction manual during assembly, the item won't work, or there are parts left over that are needed to insure proper functioning of the item. It is the same in life. Too often, we ignore the Bible—our instruction manual for living—thinking that we know how to put our lives together. Sometimes we can get along for a while without much trouble, but eventually, if we ignore the Bible's important role in providing instructions for life, we will run into difficulties. Our lives don't seem to work right. We make mistakes, and sin causes problems. In order to make sure that we live our lives the way God intended, we need to regularly read and study God's Word—His instruction manual for our lives.**

Discussion Questions

1. According to 2 Timothy 3:16-17, what are the purposes for studying Scripture? What does each of the purposes mean?

2. If the Bible is truly God's instruction manual for living, why do so many Christians struggle to read it on a regular basis?

3. What is your number-one reason for not reading and studying the Bible more often?

4. What, in your life, would you be willing to change in order to spend more time reading and studying the Bible?

Possible Topics

Importance of the Bible; the Bible as God's Word

Scripture Passages

Psalm 119:1-3,9-11,24,35,89-93,97-105,133; 1 Thessalonians 2:13; 2 Timothy 3:16-17; Hebrews 4:12-13; 2 Peter 1:3-4

Hurting on the Inside

The Big Idea

It is hard to tell from outward appearances who is hurting. God calls us to look beyond appearances and carry one another's burdens.

Materials Needed

❑ Two bananas

Preparation

Just before presenting the lesson, carefully mash the insides of one of the bananas without breaking the peel. The goal is to bruise the insides of one banana while keeping both bananas looking the same outside. This will demonstrate that although the bananas may look the same on the outside, they are radically different on the inside.

Show the two bananas, noting that they look pretty much the same. They both look like they taste really good and would be a great snack. Open the good banana and show it to the students. Then open the bruised banana and show that it is badly bruised on the inside even though it looks fine on the outside. Share the following verse:

Carry each other's burdens, and in this way you fulfill the law of Christ (Galatians 6:2).

Explain: **Most people do a good job of looking as though everything is going okay in their lives. The reality though is that many people are hurting. As Christians, we are called to carry one another's burdens, coming alongside each other for encouragement and support. Through building and deepening relationships with one another, we are able to see what is really going on in each other's lives and care for each other.**

Discussion Questions

1. How can you identify when someone is hurting?

2. What are some ways that you can fulfill the command to "carry each other's burdens"?

3. How does encouragement help someone who is facing a difficult situation?

4. How has someone encouraged you when you were feeling bruised or overburdened?

Possible Topics

Helping friends in crisis; encouraging others; relationship building

Scripture Passages

Ecclesiastes 4:9-12; John 15:12; Romans 1:12; 15:1-2; 1 Corinthians 12:26; Ephesians 4:29; 1 Thessalonians 3:2-3; Hebrews 3:13; 10:25; James 5:16

The Ice Cream Cone

The Big Idea

When we resist following Jesus and follow our own ways, we waste our lives.

Materials Needed

❑ An ice cream cone (or bar) for each student and leader

This would be a great hot-weather activity. Declare it an ice cream cone event and hand out ice cream cones to everyone, reserving one for yourself. Have everyone sit down, and begin to talk about what it means to serve Jesus. As they eat and you talk, let the cone melt over your hand and onto the floor. Make no effort to stop it, to clean it up or to keep the drips off the floor. (If you have carpet on the floor, you might want to stand with your hand over a table or a chair unless you really want the church custodian on your case!) Students will bring attention to your plight, but ignore them. Simply continue on and let it melt. **Note:** To hasten the effect, you can sit with a fan blowing on your hand—moving air (and hot weather!) will help the ice cream melt faster.

After your ice cream cone has melted, explain: **Just as I let this ice cream cone melt, so we can let our lives and opportunities melt away. The choice is ours. Will we take the opportunities that God offers us in life, or will we simply let them melt away and miss the wonderful things God has to offer? Everyone here took the opportunity to enjoy the ice cream except me.** Point out that they (hopefully) tried to tell you to eat the ice cream before it melted, but you just let it melt. Relate their comments to how others—parents, teachers, friends, youth leaders—try to encourage us when we are missing an opportunity, and that we need to listen to the encouragement of others.

Discussion Questions

1. What are ways that we often waste our lives?

2. How can we use our time wisely?

3. What are the most important activities in your schedule? Which ones might be wasting too much of your valuable time?

4. How can we know God's will for our lives?

Possible Topics

Making the best use of time; time as a valuable resource; discerning God's will for our lives; investing our God-given gifts (or His gift of time)

Scripture Passages

Psalm 31:14-15; Ecclesiastes 3:1-8; 8:5; Matthew 25:14-30; Galatians 6:9; Ephesians 5:15-17

Important Functions

The Big Idea

Each person has a valuable function in the Church—the Body of Christ—and is designed for performing specific tasks.

Materials Needed

❑ A surgical instrument (scalpel, clamp, suture, surgical tool, etc.)

Preparation

Borrow the surgical instrument from a doctor, nurse or surgical-instrument salesperson. This instrument can be small or large, but make sure that it has a significant use. Be sure you understand what the instrument is used for.

Display the surgical instrument and explain what it is and what it does. Make the point that the instrument, though it may be small and ordinary (or other characteristic), has an important function. It can't be used for another purpose during surgery because it is designed for a specific function. Share the following verse:

> **The eye cannot say to the hand, "I don't need you!" And the head cannot say to the feet, "I don't need you!" On the contrary, those parts of the body that seem to be weaker are indispensable (1 Corinthians 12:21-22).**

Explain the importance of each person's contribution to the Church—the Body of Christ. Make the point that each person has different skills and gifts that can be used to serve in specific ways. Each person is vitally important in helping the Body of Christ to function effectively.

Discussion Questions

1. Name two skills or abilities that you have.

2. Name two skills or tasks that you enjoy.

3. How can these skills and abilities be used to help strengthen, equip and/or encourage the Church—the Body of Christ?

4. If you could attempt anything for God and you were assured that you would not fail, what would you want to do?

Possible Topics

The functions of the various members of the Body of Christ; spiritual gifts; value of each person

Scripture Passages

Romans 12:3-8; 1 Corinthians 7:7; 12:1-31; 1 Peter 4:10

The Importance of Roots

The Big Idea

A well-developed spiritual root system is important for spiritually healthy growth.

Materials Needed

❑ Two identical, healthy, potted flowering plants

Preparation

About a week before the lesson, remove one plant from the pot. Cut off all of the root system leaving only the foliage and flowers; then repot the plant. Allow time for the foliage and flowers to wither.

Display the potted plants. Explain: **I bought these identical plants on the same day, but one is healthy and the other is dead.** Show students that both are in the same kind of pots; both have been given the same amount of water; and both have been placed side by side, receiving equal amounts of heat and light. Ask them what they think the problem is. Then reveal the problem of the dead plant by pulling it out of the soil. Then pull the healthy plant out of its pot, revealing the healthy root system. Share the parable of the sower in Matthew 13:1-23, especially emphasizing the following:

> **But since he has no root, he lasts only a short time. When trouble or persecution comes because of the word, he quickly falls away (Matthew 13:21).**

Explain: **Just as a healthy root system is necessary for a plant's survival, so a healthy root system is necessary for our spiritual survival.** Discuss: **What do we need to do to develop our own healthy, spiritual root systems?**

Discussion Questions

1. On a scale of 1 to 5 (1 being unhealthy and 5 being healthy), rate the status of your own spiritual root system. Explain the reasons for rating yourself as you did.

2. What issue in your life currently presents the biggest threat to your spiritual root system?

3. What are some steps you can take this week to strengthen your spiritual root system?

Possible Topics

Abiding in Christ; building a strong spiritual root system; the importance of spiritual disciplines (Bible study, prayer, worship, fellowship with believers, etc.)

Scripture Passages

Matthew 13:1-23; John 15:1-8; Romans 12:1; Ephesians 3:16-19; 5:15-20; 6:18; Colossians 2:6-7; 2 Timothy 3:16-17; Hebrews 10:24-25; James 5:16

Is That a House?

The Big Idea

What kind of foundation are you building your life upon?

Materials Needed

- ❑ Three (or more) pieces of poster board
- ❑ Three (or more) paper grocery bags
- ❑ One (or more) deck of playing cards
- ❑ Legos or Tinkertoys
- ❑ Miscellaneous items that could be put together to form a structure

Preparation

Before the meeting, fill each paper bag with one of the following items:

Bag 1—the deck of playing cards

Bag 2—a miscellaneous collection of items that really does not match

Bag 3—Legos or Tinkertoys

Note: If you have a large group, you may need to prepare more bags with the same mix of items so that when you form teams there aren't over 10 to 12 in a group.

Have students form three teams. Have each team sit around a piece of poster board. Instruct them to use the contents of their bags to build a house on the poster board.

Give a time limit of 5 to 10 minutes. When the time is up, walk around to each group and talk about each of the houses. Discuss their sturdiness, their structure, the students' creativity and, most importantly, the ability of the various houses to stand up under pressure.

Have a volunteer read aloud Matthew 7:24-27. Using the discussion questions, lead the students in a discussion about the foundation God wants us to build for our lives.

Discussion Questions

1. Which of these houses is more like the house on the sand?

2. Which of these houses is more like the house on the good foundation?

3. What made the difference between the houses?

4. According to Matthew 7:24-27, what makes the difference in our lives?

5. How do we hear God's words?

6. How do we put them into practice?

7. Which of these houses best represents your life and its foundation?

Possible Topics

Building a foundation for living; following Christ; listening to God; being obedient

Scripture Passages

Matthew 7:24-27; 1 Corinthians 3:10-17; Ephesians 2:19-22; 1 Peter 2:4-6

The Old Made New

The Big Idea

God is able to make us into new creations.

Materials Needed

❑ A piece of furniture that has been refinished (a picture of its "before" state would be a good idea) or two pieces of furniture with one in the old state and the other already refinished

Explain: **In 2 Corinthians 5:17 Paul says, "Therefore, if anyone is in Christ, he is a new creation; the old has gone, the new has come!" This refinished piece of furniture is like that—an old creation made new.** Discuss the process of refinishing, including the following key elements of the process, to explain how we become new through Him:

- Stripping away the old—Romans 6:1-4,11-14
- Sanding and buffing to make it smooth—Jeremiah 9:7
- Staining or painting to give it the final look—Galatians 5:16-25

> **Note:** A youth speaker once refinished a piece of furniture over the period of a weekend retreat. The students were involved and were really able to see the message come to life. If you are lucky enough to have a volunteer who refinishes furniture as a job or a hobby, they might be willing to do the work while someone else leads the talk.

As you, or the other person you have enlisted, either explains the process or actually refinishes the piece of furniture, explain: **This is exactly what God does with us as believers. He takes us as we are and rescues us from the trash** (death). **Jesus Christ's death and resurrection is the agent He uses to strip off our old selves** (realization of sin and conversion). **Then He sands us clean of our old sin nature** (difficulties and discipline). **After that God remakes us into new creations—what He originally intended us to be—just as a furniture refinisher uses stain or paint to restore the original beauty to furniture.**

Give students a few minutes to reflect on how God is dealing with them right now. You might ask them to share where they think they are in God's refinishing process.

Discussion Questions

1. Give an example of how having a relationship with Christ has made you a different person.

2. If you have been a Christian for a long time, how has your life become more Christlike over the years?

3. What sin issue do you struggle with that you would like God to strip away from your life?

4. If you could be more like Christ in one way, what would it be?

Possible Topics

New creation in Christ; putting off old ways; God refines and disciplines His children

Scripture Passages

Jeremiah 9:7; Zechariah 3:3-4; Romans 6:1-4,11-14; 8:1-9; 12:1-2; 2 Corinthians 5:17; Galatians 5:16-25; Hebrews 12:7-11

Only One Key
Opens the Lock

The Big Idea

Just as there is only one key that will open a given lock, there is only one way to God—through faith in Jesus Christ.

Materials Needed

❑ A padlock

❑ The key that works in the padlock

❑ Other keys that don't work—try to find at least some keys that look similar to the key that opens the padlock

Show the padlock and a key that doesn't work. Ask students if they believe that the key will open the lock. Demonstrate that the key doesn't work. Explain: **No matter how sincere we are and how deeply we believe that this particular key will open the lock, it still won't open the lock.** Try the other keys that won't work. Finally, select the key that opens the lock and open it. Read the following:

> **Jesus answered, "I am the way and the truth and the life. No one comes to the Father except through me" (John 14:6).**

Explain: **We can believe that a key will open a lock but that belief in itself will not open the lock. No matter how deeply someone believes that a certain key will open a lock, it must be the correct key in order to open the lock. Some keys look like they might open the lock, but they still don't work. Finding the correct key can be compared to finding God. A saving faith is more than just believing that God exists. True faith must be placed in the right Person. No matter how sincere someone may be or how sure they are that their good works will get them into heaven, a faith in the wrong "key" will not open the correct door. The Bible teaches that saving faith is based on belief in Jesus Christ alone.**

Discussion Questions

1. What would you say to someone who believes that there are many ways to God and that Christianity is just one of those many ways?

2. How would you respond to someone who rejects Christianity because it seems too exclusive to require people to believe in Jesus in order to get into heaven?

Possible Topics

The key to salvation; Jesus as the *only* Way to God; Christianity versus other religions

Scripture Passages

Proverbs 14:12; John 3:16-18; 14:6; Acts 4:12; 16:31; 1 John 5:11-12

The Poisoned Piñata

The Big Idea

No matter how hard we may try to hide it, our sin can't be hidden from God.

Materials Needed

- ❏ A piñata
- ❏ Garbage (coffee grounds, egg shells, fruit rinds, etc.)
- ❏ A stick or bat
- ❏ A blindfold
- ❏ A plastic drop cloth
- ❏ **Optional:** Another piñata filled with candy

Preparation

Advertise the meeting for a few weeks before the big event, highlighting the piñata theme and the great fun and treats to be had. Before the meeting, fill the piñata with the garbage and set it up over the drop cloth (or set this up outside). **Option:** Also prepare a second piñata filled with candy (or at least bring candy to give to students after the lesson).

As the meeting begins, act excited and let students believe that there's some great stuff inside the piñata. Blindfold the first batter and let him or her have a few swings at the piñata. As more batters take their turns and the piñata breaks, students will dive for the treats before they realize that the piñata's bounty is really garbage. Discuss: **Were you surprised by what came out of the piñata?** Explain that people can be similar to this piñata; they can work hard to look like committed Christians, but on the inside they aren't committed to Jesus at all. Ask volunteers to share about a time when they've gone through the motions of looking like a *good* Christian, but their hearts weren't where they should have been.

Possible Topics

Hidden sin; professing to know Christ but denying Him with our actions

Scripture Passages

Matthew 7:15-23; 23:27-28; Titus 1:16; 1 John 1:6,8; 2:4

The Power of Habits— Good and Bad

The Big Idea

Over time, behaviors turn into habits and become difficult to change. God has the power to overcome our bad habits and set us free.

Materials Needed

☐ A spool of thread

☐ Scissors

Choose a student volunteer—this is most effective with an athletic type—and wrap a single thread once around the student, across the arms and tie the thread. Instruct the volunteer to break free, which will be easy to do. Next, wrap the thread three times around the student and tie it. Ask the volunteer to break free. It will be more difficult to break free, but he or she should be able to do it. Repeat this exercise wrapping more and more thread around the student until he or she is no longer able to break free. When the volunteer cannot break free, use the scissors to cut him or her free. Share the following verse:

> **Don't you know that when you offer yourselves to someone to obey him as slaves, you are slaves to the one whom you obey—whether you are slaves to sin, which leads to death, or to obedience, which leads to righteousness? (Romans 6:16).**

Explain: **Habits—whether good or bad—are formed by repetition. In the beginning, habits are easier to break. But with repetition and time, habits become more and more difficult to break. Let this demonstration be a reminder that bad habits are harmful to you and hard to break, but also let it be an encouragement to you to form good habits such as daily Scripture reading and prayer.** Be sure to make the point that God can set us free from bad habits in the same way that you cut the student free with the scissors.

Discussion Questions

1. Does anyone intentionally set out to develop a bad habit? Why do we develop bad habits even when we know they are harmful?

2. What are some common sinful habits that people develop?

3. Which of these common sinful habits are easy to break and which ones are difficult?

4. What advice would you give to someone who wanted to break a bad habit?

Possible Topics

Habits; the power of sin; God's power to change lives

Scripture Passages

Romans 6:18; 7:15-20; 1 Corinthians 6:12; Galatians 5:1; Philippians 4:13; Hebrews 12:1-2; James 1:13-15; 2 Peter 2:19; 1 John 1:6-10

Real Faith Requires Taking Risks

The Big Idea

Real faith requires not only belief, but actions based on that belief.

Materials Needed

❑ A 15-foot length of rope
❑ Two stepladders

Lay the rope on the floor in a straight line. Ask for a volunteer who is willing to help you (be sure to select someone won't be crazy enough to try to walk the aboveground tightrope!). Instruct the volunteer to walk the rope—tightrope-style—on the floor. The volunteer will (hopefully!) do this with no problem. Keep the volunteer up front with you. Bring out the stepladders and place one at each end of the rope on the floor. Ask for two strong volunteers. Instruct them to each pick up one end of the rope and secure the end to the top of their assigned stepladder, making an aboveground tightrope. Now ask the original volunteer if he or she is willing to walk across the rope again. When the student declines, have all volunteers sit down. Share the following:

> **What good is it, my brothers, if a man claims to have faith but has no deeds? Can such faith save him? (James 2:14).**

Explain: **Walking a tightrope placed on the floor is easy because there's no risk. Walking a tightrope off the ground is entirely different. When the risk factor is added, most people won't attempt it. Having faith in Jesus is a lot like walking on that tightrope. Many people find it easy to believe in Jesus when there is no risk involved—when nothing is asked or expected of them. Real faith requires action, not just belief. Real faith is displayed even when believing in Jesus gets hard. Real faith is shown when friends reject you because you believe in Jesus, and you keep believing anyway. Real faith is shown when you turn the other cheek when you are put down, hurt or persecuted by others. Real faith is showing love to someone who is unpopular or disliked simply in spite of the fact that you might be ridiculed by others. Belief plus action equals real faith!**

Dr. Tony Campolo tells the story of Blondin, a tightrope walker in the 1800s who strung a tightrope across the Niagara Falls. Read the following story:

> Before ten thousand screaming people [Blondin] inched his way from the Canadian side of the falls to the United States side. When he got there, the crowd began shouting his name: "Blondin! Blondin! Blondin! Blondin!"
>
> Finally he raised his arms, quieted the crowd and shouted to them, "I am Blondin! Do you believe in me?"
>
> The crowd shouted back, "We believe! We believe! We believe!"
>
> Again he quieted the crowd, and once more he shouted to them, "I'm going back across the tightrope, but this time I'm going to carry someone on my back. Do you believe I can do that?"
>
> The crowd yelled, "We believe! We believe!"
>
> He quieted them one more time and then he asked, "Who will be that person?" The crowd went silent. Nothing.
>
> Finally, out of the crowd stepped one man. He climbed on Blondin's shoulders, and for the next three-and-a-half hours, Blondin inched his way back across the tightrope to the Canadian side of the falls.[1]

Conclude by explaining: **The point of the story is that 10,000 people stood there that day, chanting, "We believe, we believe!" but only one person really believed enough to volunteer to be carried across on Blondin's back. Believing is not just saying, "I accept the fact." Believing is giving your life over into the hands of the one in whom you say you believe.**

Christ calls us to step out of our comfort zones and walk with Him. Stepping out on faith means that you don't know all that is going to happen, but you are putting your trust in the One who does. Putting your trust in Jesus is not usually the easy or comfortable way to go. The risk is doing what seems humanly impossible by trusting God who is all knowing and all powerful. He holds the future in His hands. Are you ready to take a step in the direction of faith? Then accept God's challenge to act on faithful obedience—to be a doer of His word, not merely a listener (see James 1:22).

Discussion Questions

1. When is it hardest for you to believe in God? When is it easiest?

2. Give an example of a time when you have taken a risk that demonstrated your faith in Jesus.

3. What is one difficult action that you need to step out and do to show your faith in God's trustworthiness?

Possible Topics

Real faith; taking risks for God; faith and works

Scripture Passages

2 Thessalonians 1:4,11; 1 Timothy 6:11-12; James 1:22; 2:14-26

Note

1. Tony Campolo, *You Can Make a Difference* (Waco, TX: Word, 1984), p. 14.

The Real You

The Big Idea

Words and actions reflect the spiritual condition of the heart.

Materials Needed

❑ A clear drinking glass, half filled with water

Begin by pointing out that many Christians act one way when they're at church or church-related activities and act another way when they're at school or with friends who don't go to church. Facilitate a brief discussion using the following questions:

- Has there been a time when you acted differently around your non-Christian friends than you would act around your Christian friends?
- What causes us to act differently in different situations?
- In what situations are you most tempted to act differently?

Allow for a few responses; then have students silently consider the following question: **When someone's behavior changes depending upon the people around him or her, which of his or her behaviors reflect the real person inside?**

Hold up the glass and pour some water out onto the floor. Ask: **Why did water spill on the floor?** Allow for a few responses; then point out that the main reason that water spilled from the glass is because there was water in the glass to begin with. Use this illustration to make the following connection: **The words we say and the actions we take reflect who we really are inside.**

Explain that our words and actions reveal the condition of our hearts. Challenge students to look up the Scripture passages listed and to take time to examine their lives, searching for who they are inside. Explain: **No one is perfect. God knows that, but He wants us to admit to ourselves where we are in our lives. He does not want us to be phony or try to hide ourselves from Him. Confessing our faults and sins to God is the most important step for cleaning out the junk in our lives. When we confess our sins, we can know for sure that God will forgive us and restore us to a right relationship with Him.**

Possible Topics

Hypocrisy; self-discovery; relationship with God; God's forgiveness

Scripture Passages

Jeremiah 17:9; Matthew 15:18-19; Luke 6:43-45; 1 John 1:8-9

Soft Gospel

The Big Idea

Making the message of Jesus easy to digest and acceptable is not a benefit in terms of human spiritual needs, but actually a deterrent to helping others.

Materials Needed

- ❑ Lots of coins
- ❑ A glass jar with a screw-on lid
- ❑ Several pillows/cushions
- ❑ A tarp
- ❑ Index cards
- ❑ Pens or pencils

Preparation

Put the coins in a pint-sized mayonnaise or similar jar—one with a top that screws on tightly. Have a good mix of several different sizes of coins. Have a wide and thick pile of pillows ready, stacked deep. You will be tossing the jar on the pillows, so make sure it's very deep. Also set up a tarp in an area where you will be shattering the jar. Place this area far enough away from the students to insure safety when you break the jar.

Explain that that there are certain things that all human beings need. Ask for a few volunteers who will write down student responses, and give them index cards and pens or pencils. Ask students to call out what these needs are; for example, air, water, food, love, sense of belonging, the forgiveness of sins, a relationship with God, peace, etc. As the needs are suggested, have the volunteers write them on index cards and put them on the pillows.

Display the jar of coins and tell them that the coins represent God's desire to provide for the needs of all humans, but that they have become encased in the hard glass jar of human sin.

Drop the jar on the pillows and remark that God's answers are not getting through to the needs of people. With the volunteers' help, move the *needs* cards to the tarp, have everyone stand back a good safe distance and *drop* the jar on the tarp, allowing it to shatter. **Note:** Don't throw the jar down; gravity will do the job, and throwing it has the potential for shards of glass to travel dangerously far.

Discuss how being soft Christians who present a soft gospel can deceive people into thinking they can accept the Lord and then go do what they want. We need to present the hard truths of the gospel and the promise that Christ changes lives and forgives sins. Talk about the difference between a soft gospel that makes it sound easy to follow Jesus and makes people think that anyone can be a believer on his or her own terms, and the true gospel that tells about our sin, our need for a Savior and that we must deny ourselves, pick up our crosses daily and follow Him.

Challenge students to become devoted to the truth and to live their relationship with God before a lost and hurting world. Suggest that Christians are like the mayonnaise jar; we need to be broken by the impact of our own sin before we can have any effect on the world around us.

Discussion Questions

1. What are some examples of Christians being too soft and watering down the gospel?

2. What is the gospel of Jesus?

3. Why is living Christ's way so important?

4. How can we, as a youth group, be more straightforward in our faith by meeting just one of the needs discussed tonight? Challenge students to choose a community need that was suggested, and, plan, as a group, a way to meet that need.

Possible Topics

Mission; evangelism; radical living for Christ

Scripture Passages

Matthew 10:37-39; 25:31-45; Luke 9:23-26; 14:25-35

Spiritual Pride Is a Trap

The Big Idea

Something that looks impossible can happen. When spiritual strength leads to pride, people become vulnerable to sin.

Materials Needed

- ❏ One hard-boiled egg, peeled
- ❏ A glass milk bottle
- ❏ Two matches

Preparation

Before the lesson, boil an egg and peel it. Make sure that it is large enough to sit on top of the empty milk bottle without falling in.

Place the egg on top of the bottle. Confidently state the obvious: **This egg doesn't look like it can fall into the bottle.** Take the egg off the top of the milk bottle and then light both matches and drop them into the milk bottle. Immediately replace the egg on top of the milk bottle. The matches will burn up the oxygen in the milk bottle, creating a vacuum which will then suck the egg into the bottle.

Explain as you are waiting for the egg to fall into the bottle: **At times we believe we are so spiritually strong that we are invulnerable to Satan's traps. Pride creeps in and we might say, "There's no way I would ever do that" in regard to behaviors— especially addictive behaviors such as sexual promiscuity, drugs, alcohol, gambling, etc. This is a dangerous thing to believe. Spiritual pride is a trap that Satan sets for us. Just when we think we can't fall, we become most susceptible to falling. Be on guard against pride!**

Discussion Questions

1. Is it ever possible to get to the place in your life where you don't have to worry about falling to some temptation? Why or why not?

2. What does Proverbs 16:18 mean?

3. In what ways can we help one another avoid spiritual pride?

Possible Topics

Pride/humility; spiritual accountability; Satan's wiles

Scripture Passages

Psalm 18:27; Proverbs 16:18; 29:23; Matthew 23:12; Luke 14:11; Galatians 6:1; James 3:13; 4:6-10; 1 Peter 5:5-9

What You See Is Not Always What You Get

The Big Idea

People often make poor judgments about others based on first impressions. We must be careful to look beyond first impressions, because what we see initially is not always the whole story.

Materials Needed

❑ A (clean!) litter box

❑ A cat litter pooper-scooper (also clean)

❑ Boxes of Grape Nuts

❑ Six thick, stubby Tootsie Rolls

Preparation

This object lesson will work best in a home setting. Done correctly, it is an object lesson your students will probably never forget. Before the lesson, fill the litter box about half full with Grape Nuts. Next, microwave the Tootsie Rolls until they become soft enough to mold into the shape of well, let's just call them "litter box snacks." For added effect, while the shaped Tootsie Rolls are warm, roll them around in the Grape Nuts to get some of them to stick. Then place the shaped Tootsie Rolls in strategic places in the litter box with some buried and some sticking up above the Grape Nuts. The goal here is to make it look like a real, well-used litter box.

Bring the litter box out for the lesson. Tell students that they all, of course, know what this object is. Using the pooper-scooper, fish a Tootsie Roll out, holding it with the scooper. Ask students how much they would pay for you to take a bite of the "litter-box snack." Some students may literally start gagging here, so work quickly before you lose your audience. Go ahead and take the challenge; you should get quite a reaction from the group. (**Option:** For those with more highly developed sensitivities, you can do a similar object lesson using a potted plant which has been placed in soil made of crushed Oreo cookies. At the appropriate time in the object lesson, eat the Oreo dirt.)

Share the following:

> But the LORD said to Samuel, "Do not consider his appearance or his height, for I have rejected him. The LORD does not look at the things man looks at. Man looks at the outward appearance, but the LORD looks at the heart" (1 Samuel 16:7).

Explain that what you just ate was really a Tootsie Roll and that they jumped to the wrong conclusion. Then explain the following application: **Some things are not what they appear to be at first glance! We often make judgments about people based on first impressions. But beware! Some people are not what they seem to be at first. Unfortunately, too often we make judgments about others based on characteristics that aren't really important. We might make judgments based on physical appearance, clothing or how outgoing, intelligent or funny someone is. But these outward signs may not be a true picture of a person's real self. God values each person because He created each one of us. He never makes a judgment based on outward appearances. He values us for who we really are on the inside. Next time you are tempted to jump to a conclusion about a person because of a poor first impression, remember the Litter-Box Snack lesson and look at others through God's eyes.**

Discussion Questions

1. Give an example of a time when you made a mistake in judging someone based on first impressions. What changed your mind?

2. Have you had an experience where someone judged you by a first impression? What happened when that person got to know you better?

3. What are the dangers of making an incorrect judgment about someone based on first impressions?

4. According to 1 Samuel 16:7, how should we judge others?

Possible Topics

First impressions; judging others; the value of a person in God's eyes

Scripture Passages

1 Samuel 16:7; Isaiah 53:2-12; Matthew 7:1-5; John 7:24; Romans 14:9-12; 15:7; Galatians 2:6; James 2:1-12; 4:12

When Candles Burn Out

The Big Idea

As Christians, we are called to be light in the dark world.

Materials Needed

- ❏ A package of birthday candles and one larger candle
- ❏ Candleholders and clay
- ❏ Lighters or matches
- ❏ Blankets/towels

Preparation

Before the meeting, time how long it will take for either a few small candles or a bunch of birthday candles to burn out. You will be talking in sync with the candles burning out.

Hold the meeting in a room that can be entirely darkened, even stuffing blankets and/or towels around doors and windows to keep light from creeping in. Turn out the lights in adjacent rooms.

Gather students in the darkened meeting room and light the birthday candles as the only illumination. Stick the candles in clay inside glass or metal candleholders and place them in the corners of the room. Have adult leaders light them simultaneously. Begin by explaining that in Christ, we as believers are His lights in a darkened world and that each of us combined with the whole Body of Christ keeps the darkness at bay. Read verses on light while the candles burn lower.

As the candles begin to sputter out, shift the talk to those who don't know God and, more importantly, those who refuse and reject God. When the darkness is complete, ask the students to get up and to slowly move about the room. Have adult advisors quickly set some obstacles in the way, putting some things on the floor that make their steps different, such as sections of cardboard, plastic or even dry cereal that will crunch when stepped on. Have them set a few chairs up quickly for them to bump into. To avoid injuries, warn students to move slowly and not push. Ask them to simply move to another location in the room and sit down.

Discuss what it was like to move around in the darkness. Then suddenly light the larger candle and discuss the contrast.

Discussion Questions

1. What was it like to see the candles beginning to go out and to be gradually surrounded by darkness?

2. How did you feel when you moved around in the dark room?

3. How did you try to protect yourself as we moved about? What would it be like to always live like that?

4. How did you feel when the candle was lit and the darkness was dispelled?

Possible Topics

Life without Christ; the power of light over darkness; Christian influence; Jesus as the Light of the world

Scripture Passages

2 Samuel 22:29; Psalm 18:28; 19:8b; 27:1; 89:15; 119:105,130; Proverbs 4:18-19; Isaiah 9:2; 60:1-3,19-20; Micah 7:8-9; Matthew 4:16; 5:14-16; 6:22-23; Luke 8:16-17; John 1:4-5,9; 3:19-21; 8:12; 12:46; Romans 13:12; 2 Corinthians 4:6; Ephesians 5:8-14; 1 Thessalonians 5:4-6; 1 Peter 2:9; 1 John 1:5-7; 2:8-11

Where Am I Going?

The Big Idea

We can know where we are, spiritually, through the study of God's Word.

Materials Needed

❑ A handheld Global Positioning System (GPS) unit—you shouldn't have too much trouble finding or renting one

Invite students to share a recent experience where they got lost. You might explain a personal experience to get them started. Discuss the frustration of being lost. Then show the GPS unit. Demonstrate that it works by receiving signals from satellites orbiting the Earth. Explain: **This GPS unit can keep track of where you are anywhere in the world. With a GPS you can always know where you are going, and you should never be lost.**

The Bible—God's Word—is our spiritual GPS unit! God has assured us in His Word that we can have eternal life, and when we read and study the Bible, we will learn how to navigate through this life. With the Bible as our guide, we will never be lost!

Discussion Questions

1. Have you ever doubted that you are really a Christian? If so, what caused your doubt?

2. According to 1 John 5:11-13, how can you know whether or not you have eternal life?

3. How does the Bible serve as a guide for life?

4. How do you think your life would be different if you consulted the Bible more often?

Possible Topics

Assurance of salvation; guidance for living; the value of the Bible

Scripture Passages

2 Timothy 3:16-17; Hebrews 4:12-13; 1 John 5:11-13

The Windows of Our Soul

The Big Idea

When our efforts don't work out, we need to evaluate what we're doing and seek God's will for our lives.

Materials Needed

❑ An old window frame with four panes of glass (available from remodeling sites, architectural recyclers or through carpenters or glaziers)

❑ A piece of clear Plexiglas (available at most hardware stores)

❑ A folding chair

❑ A foot-long piece of metal pipe

❑ A canvas drop cloth or an old blanket

Preparation

Replace one glass pane with the Plexiglas and, if needed, use dirt to make the new pane look like the old ones. Lay the drop cloth on the floor and prop the frame on the folding chair set on the drop cloth.

Discuss: **What changes need to be made when we give our lives to Christ** (our attitudes, actions, morals and values)**?** After several responses, ask: **Why do we resist the influence Jesus wants to have in our lives?** Allow for responses; then share a personal example of an area in which you struggled, such as rebellion against your parents or disobedience of a school rule. **Note:** Don't be too revealing. Often leaders make themselves out to be folk heroes when they talk about their life of sin; students might then think *My youth leader did this and it worked out OK, so I can try it too!* Be sure to relate the consequences of your wrong actions.

As you describe a time when you failed because you relied on your old ways, pick up the metal pipe and casually smash out a pane of glass from the window frame. **Caution:** You need only to tap the glass; the pipe will easily break it. The point is made through the glass breaking, not through seeing how far the glass will fly.

Continue sharing, and as you talk about wanting to do things your own way instead of God's way, use the pipe to break the second and then the third pane of glass. Discuss:

How can Christ help us to clean up the messes we've made?

Transition by sharing about how your growing faith enabled you to trust Jesus with your life, and that it was because of this trust that He began to change you. Tap the Plexiglas pane (you can hit it harder than you did the glass) and point out that when we are walking with Jesus, He will provide the strength to do God's will for our lives.

Possible Topics

New life in Christ; maturing in Christ; the lordship of Christ versus relying on self

Scripture Passages

Proverbs 3:3,5-6; Philippians 2:5; 4:13

You Are Valuable

The Big Idea

God created each of us, loves us and values us simply for who we are and not for what we have done or in spite of anything that has been done to us.

Materials Needed

❑ A $20 bill

❑ Wet dirt (just shy of being mud) in a small container

Hold the $20 bill up, showing it to students without telling them what it is. Ask them how much it is worth. Next perform the following series of actions on the bill, and after each action, ask students how much they think the bill is worth.

1. Crinkle the bill up just a bit.
2. Wad the bill up tightly in your hand; then smooth out the bill.
3. Rub it in the wet dirt.
4. Rip the bill slightly.

Finally, make the point that no matter how crumpled or dirty or torn the bill is, it is still worth $20. Read the following verse:

How great is the love the Father has lavished on us, that we should be called children of God! And that is what we are! (1 John 3:1).

Explain: **Many of us believe that we are not worth anything, especially to God. Sometimes we believe this because of the sins that we have committed. Others believe this because of the sins that others have committed against them. God loves and values each of us, no matter what we might have done or what has been done to us. God values us for who we are as His creation and children.**

Discussion Questions

1. How does your behavior affect what you believe that God thinks and feels about you?

2. How can someone else's behavior toward you have an effect on how you believe God thinks and feels about you?

3. If God were to tell someone about you, what do you think He would say?

4. What difference should God's love for you make in terms of how you think and feel about yourself?

Possible Topics

God's unconditional love; self-esteem; self-worth

Scripture Passages

Psalm 139:1-16; Jeremiah 31:3; John 8:1-11; Romans 5:6-8; 8:35-39; Ephesians 2:1-10; 1 John 3:1

Case Studies

Cindy's Driving!

Cindy was ecstatic as she stood looking at her new driver's license! She had looked forward to this moment for a long time. This was the best birthday present ever! Today was the first day that Cindy was eligible to get her driver's license, and she had taken her driver's tests and passed! It was incredible!

"Mom, can I have the car tonight?" she asked as she proudly drove home.

"Well, I suppose you can," her mother said after giving it some consideration. "But, you need to be home by nine. This is a school night, you know."

"I'll be back by nine, Mom. I promise," Cindy said as she walked out the door after dinner.

"Be careful!" her mother shouted.

After picking up a few friends, Cindy headed for the mall. Everyone was excited because Cindy was the first of their friends to get a driver's license. As the group was talking and enjoying their newfound freedom, Cindy glanced to the backseat—for just a moment—to say something to one of her friends. As she had her head turned for just that *one* moment, the car drifted to the right and slammed into a car parked on the street. Fortunately, no one was seriously hurt, but both cars were badly damaged. Cindy was afraid of what her parents might say or do.

Optional Activity: Have students act two different role-plays of what might occur. One would have the parents reacting as non-Christians and the other would have the parents reacting as Christians should.

Discussion Questions

1. How might Cindy's mom act toward Cindy in light of the car accident?

2. What does age have to do with maturity?

3. How does making mistakes affect the development of maturity?

4. How do we know when someone is mature enough to handle new responsibilities?

Possible Topics

Maturity; responsibility; decision making; consequences

Scripture Passages

Psalm 119:105; Proverbs 19:18; 1 Corinthians 13:11; James 1:2-5

Dating a Non-Christian

Jenna has been raised in a Christian home all her life. She thinks her parents are the strictest parents in the world. Now that she is 16 years old, they are finally giving her the opportunity to date, but her last conversation with them really bugged her. Jason took Jenna to their high school basketball game and then to the dance after the game. He was very polite to Jenna's parents and a gentleman toward her, and he got her home right on time. The next day Jenna's mom asked Jenna if Jason was a Christian. Jenna immediately got defensive and told her mom that it was none of her business and that he might not be a Christian, but he was very nice and that she liked him a lot.

That evening Jenna's mom and dad sat down with her after dinner and said, "We don't think you should date Jason anymore. The Bible says that Christians should not date non-Christians."

Jenna responded angrily, "Mom, you married Dad before he was a Christian, and then he became a believer. Isn't that a double standard?"

Discussion Questions

1. If you were giving advice to Jenna, what would you tell her?

2. What could her parents have done better in this situation?

3. How would you respond to this statement: "The Bible says that Christians should not date non-Christians"?

4. Second Corinthians 6:14 says, "Do not be yoked together with unbelievers. For what do righteousness and wickedness have in common? Or what fellowship can light have with darkness?" How would you relate this verse to Jenna's situation?

Possible Topics
Dating; relationships with non-Christians

Scripture Passages
2 Corinthians 6:14; Ephesians 6:1-3

Do You Hear Me?

Unbelievable. There it was—sitting right in front of him—the sound system of his dreams. It had everything, all the bells and whistles. Kevin would have never dreamed in a million years that his parents would have bought him something like this. *My parents are the best*, Kevin thought.

"Happy birthday, dear," Kevin's mom said, affection oozing from her tone of voice.

"Son, we also bought you the best earphones we could find. When your mother and I are around, please use them," Kevin's dad added.

Man, I knew there was a catch in this deal, Kevin thought. To him, it was like buying a sports car and never driving faster than 35 mph. It just wasn't right.

Within three months, the sound-system wars had already inflicted serious damage on the family's relationships. Every morning Kevin would get up and turn on the system. He only knew one volume setting: *Loud*. He needed the noise to help him wake up. His dad was just the opposite. He liked to ease into each new day with a cup of coffee, his newspaper and quiet. Each day, the same scenario seemed to play itself out. When Kevin was in the shower, his dad would go into Kevin's bedroom and turn off the system. When Kevin got back to his room, he would be angry that someone had turned the music off and he would slam his door and turn the music back on—just a bit louder to make his point. His mom would then go to Kevin's bedroom, knock on the door and yell, "Turn it down, honey! Do you hear me? Turn it down!"

Kevin could hear his mother, but ignored her. *God, why did you give me parents like this?* Kevin would wonder.

One day Kevin came home from school, and as usual he looked forward to kicking back and relaxing to some good music. His parents were always at work in the afternoon, so this was *his* time. He walked into his bedroom and he couldn't believe his eyes. The sound system was gone. Kevin was furious. He went to his parents' room, unhooked their television from the cable, took it and hid it in the attic. *Two can play at this game*, Kevin thought. Then he went back to his room and dreamed how he could trade his parents in for a new set.

When both his parents had come home from work, Kevin stormed out of his room and made his grand entrance into the kitchen. "What do you think you are doing?!" Kevin yelled. "Give it back! You have no right to go into my room without my permission, and you have absolutely no right to take my property! You thieves!"

Mom responded as calmly as she could, "Sweetie, calm down. We have every right to do what we did. We are your parents. You live in our house and you live under our rules. We love you, and we are trying to teach you responsibility."

"Give it back!" Kevin screamed.

Kevin's dad was not nearly as calm as his mother. His pointing finger communicated as much as his words. "Son, you are so ungrateful! We gave you that sound system out of the kindness of our hearts. You abused that kindness. Do you hear me?! We've asked you to be considerate. Then we told you what we expected from you. We told you that if you didn't respect our requests, we'd have to do something you wouldn't like! You have consistently ignored our wishes! We will not give the system back! We cannot give it back, because . . . we've SOLD it! We've even talked to Pastor Steve about this. He told us that if you wouldn't obey us, that we were doing the right thing by selling the system!"

Kevin's mind was racing. He couldn't believe what he was hearing. Even the youth pastor had sold him out. Kevin turned away and walked toward the back door. He turned back to his parents as he opened the door. Firmly but calmly he said, "I want it back. Oh, and by the way, Mommy and Daddy, have fun watching TV tonight." With that parting shot, he walked out and slammed the door.

Discussion Questions

1. Which of the characters in the story do you consider to be the most at fault in this situation? Why?

2. What could have been done to prevent the conflict from becoming so severe?

3. How could we express disagreement with our parents in a way that still shows honor and respect?

4. What are steps we can take to improve communication between us and our parents?

Possible Topics
Family relationships; handling conflict; communication

Scripture Passages
Proverbs 12:18; Ephesians 6:1-3; Philippians 2:4; Colossians 3:12-17,20-21

A Driving Dilemma

In Jake's home state, a study was conducted that showed a dramatic decrease in accidents for newly licensed drivers when the new drivers were prevented by law from driving with passengers under the age of 18 for the first six months after being licensed. Most of Jake's friends are driving, and he can't wait to get his driver's license when he turns 16 in a few months.

Most of Jake's friends don't take the mandated six-month probationary period seriously. They drive their friends all around, some doing it without their parents' knowledge and some with their parents' permission "as long as they drive safely." Jake's parents have told him that he is absolutely forbidden to ride in a car with anyone driving who has not already passed the six-month period. They've warned him that if he disobeys them and gets caught, he will not be allowed to get *his* license when he turns 16. Jake thinks his parents are far too strict, and he still takes rides sometimes from his friends who are probationary drivers.

Discussion Questions

1. Are Jake's parent's too strict?

2. Is Jake wrong to drive with his friends?

3. As Jake's friend, what would you say to him?

Possible Topics

Temptation; peer pressure; friendships; handling conflict; respect; relationship with parents; communication

Scripture Passages

Ephesians 6:1; Colossians 3:20; 1 Corinthians 15:33

Faith Crisis

Justin was a really good guy from a strong Christian family. He didn't drink, party or do much of anything wrong outside of an occasional argument with his parents. He couldn't remember a time in his life when he didn't believe in God. He loved his youth group and had volunteered to help with mission projects. Most people viewed Justin as a really strong Christian.

Justin had a major problem; he was beginning to face very powerful doubts about the existence of God. He felt that when he prayed nothing happened. He didn't see God answering his prayers. As he looked around the church he had attended his whole life, he began to see hypocrites in the congregation and he questioned God's presence in their lives. At school, Justin's science teacher taught things that were completely contrary to what the Bible said, and the more he listened to his teacher, the more confused Justin became.

Justin began to realize that he might be going through something he had heard of called a faith crisis. He wanted to believe, but the doubts just kept creeping in. Not wanting to upset his parents, Justin kept going to church, but he was becoming more bored each time he went.

Discussion Questions

1. What should Justin do?

2. What verses from Scripture would you share with him to help with his questions?

3. Is it good to struggle with doubts? Why or why not?

Possible Topics

Doubt; faith; the existence of God

Scripture Passages

John 20:27; Hebrews 11:1-6; James 1:5-8; Jude 22

Influencing Others

The youth pastor, Bob, thought the guys in his high school youth group were finally getting their act together. The guys were actually welcoming to others and trying to get to know the new students who were attending. One new student, Mike, began attending church because his mother had found religion and hoped that her son would also benefit. Up to this point in his life, Mike hadn't really heard much or, at least, paid much notice to who Jesus was. Pastor Bob was really encouraged that Mike was very open to hearing and talking about Jesus. And Bob thought it was a good sign when three of his regular youth-group guys—all professing Christians and from solid Christian backgrounds—welcomed Mike and began to include him as part of their group of friends.

About a month later, these four young men—led by one of the regular youth-group guys—were arrested on felony charges after discharging explosives and lighting gasoline on and around a disliked teacher's home. What had begun as random pranks evolved into a trail of vandalism and arson.

After his arrest, Mike was cleared of charges. He had cooperated with police and had not been significantly involved in the crimes. It seemed as though he had gotten innocently involved with the wrong people. He never returned to church. He never returned Bob's phone calls.

Discussion Questions

1. What are your thoughts about this story?

2. Why do you think Mike cut his connection with the church and Pastor Bob?

3. What responsibilities do Christian students have in supporting and building up other Christian students?

4. What are our responsibilities as Christians to students who are not yet believers?

Possible Topics

Influencing others; lifestyle as a witness—for better or worse; responsibility to care for other people

Scripture Passages

Matthew 18:6-9; Romans 14:13; 15:1-2; 1 Corinthians 10:24,32-33; Philippians 2:4

Is There Really Any Difference?

Jason was a well-rounded guy, a good kid. He did a little bit of everything. He made good grades, played most sports well and played a musical instrument. He even helped out at a local homeless shelter.

One day at lunch, Jason and some friends were talking about life and what they wanted to do when they graduated. Jason said to his friends, "I think I would like to do some mission work in Juarez, Mexico, where I went last summer."

His friends starting laughing and joking with him about how silly that would be. One friend said, "Jason, that sounds like something one of those geeky Christians would say, and you are not one of those." Jason just laughed along and left without saying another word.

That night Jason struggled with doubts and questions. Why did his friends not know he was a Christian? Why did they think Christians were geeky? What was a Christian guy supposed to do? Wasn't he different from his friends? He sat down and began to list how he was different from them.

- When everyone else was telling dirty jokes, he just listened; he didn't tell them.
- He had never used someone else's homework to copy. In fact he was the nice guy who let others use his homework.
- At parties he did not drink alcohol. He drank a soda.
- He had made out with a few girls, but he had never gone all the way. (Although some might think he had from the way he had left out a few details.)

Discussion Questions

1. What conclusion do you think Jason came to that night?

2. Was Jason really any different from his non-Christian friends? If so, how?

3. Did his life reflect the difference God had made in it? Explain your answer.

4. What might be the answers to Jason's questions?

5. What are some steps Jason could take to right this situation and to help others see Christ in him?

6. How do you relate to Jason? What steps will you take to make the necessary changes in your lifestyle?

Possible Topics

Authentic Christianity; how Christians should be different; lifestyle evangelism

Scripture Passages

Matthew 5:14-16; 10:32-33; Mark 8:34-38; Luke 9:26; Romans 1:16; 10:14-15; Colossians 3:1-10,12-17; 1 Timothy 1:8-9; 1 Peter 3:13-16

The Love Letter

Todd and Sarah were college students who met during summer vacation while working at a resort. They started off by saying hello whenever they saw each other. Todd finally got up the courage to ask Sarah out for a date, and the romance began. Todd and Sarah would spend their days off together at the beach, taking long walks or going out to get something to eat. They were both in love; they could see it in each other's eyes. Yet, Todd was shy and had a hard time expressing his feelings with words.

The summer quickly passed and the cool fall breezes meant that it was time for Todd to fly home, so Sarah took him to the airport. They spent a long time embracing as tears welled up in their eyes. Would they ever see each other again? Finally it was time for Todd to board the plane—he had to go. He pulled an envelope out of his pocket and gave it to Sarah. Her name was on it. Todd turned and walked slowly away as Sarah cried. She put the envelope in her purse and headed for her car.

Sarah was terribly depressed; Todd was gone. She stopped at a restaurant and ordered lunch. Sitting at the table, she took the envelope out of her purse and looked it over. When the waitress brought the food, she put the envelope away—she wasn't sure she wanted to read it anyway. Lunch was okay, but nothing tasted as good anymore; Todd was gone. If only she could hear his voice right now; but she couldn't.

When Sarah got home, she turned on the television. She couldn't find a program that interested her, but she watched a soap opera anyway. She figured she might as well be depressed by someone else's problems instead of her own. But no matter what she did, Sarah could not chase away the reality that Todd was gone. She loved him so much. What would she do without him? During a commercial, she remembered the envelope.

Turning off the television, she took the letter out of her purse and looked at the outside of the envelope once again, wondering what he might have written. She missed Todd so much; she felt so empty. The shrill ring of the telephone broke the silence. Putting the envelope down, Sarah answered the phone. It was her friend Willa, asking if Sarah would go to the mall with her. Willa knew that Sarah would be feeling bad, so she figured this would get her mind off of Todd being gone. Knowing she should get out, Sarah agreed to go and glanced at the envelope as she went out the door. *Oh, if we could only be together*, she thought.

Days went by and nothing cheered Sarah up; Todd was gone. It was almost like he had died. Occasionally, Sarah would pick up the envelope that Todd had addressed to her and look at it, but she never opened it. It just made her sad, and it seemed that something always got in the way. *Why hasn't Todd called me?* Sarah wondered. *He must not really love me or else he would call me.*

Weeks went by and Sarah was starting to resent Todd. *He doesn't care about me*, she thought. *What a jerk I was to believe that he loved me.* She looked for the envelope and found it under a pile of bills and papers. It was rumpled now—wrinkled and stained by a coffee spill. "Todd, where are you?" she cried as she threw the envelope across the room. It landed in a corner.

Months later, Sarah found the envelope, still lying in the corner. She picked it up and put it in the trash. The letter she never opened had said:

Dear Sarah:

Though these words have not yet been said, they have now long been true.

These words will closely bond us although they are few,

They can never be broken, wherever I am, or whatever you do.

My Sarah, my dear Sarah, nothing else matters than this—

"I Love You."

Will you marry me?

Please reply.

Todd

Discussion Questions

1. Describe your thoughts and feelings about Sarah's not opening Todd's letter. What did she miss out on because she did not read the letter?

2. How is this story similar to people who say they want to know God but won't read the Bible?

3. What reasons do people have for not reading the Bible?

4. How can you overcome the obstacles that keep you from reading God's Word more often?

Possible Topics

The Bible is God's love letter to us; spending time with God; discipleship

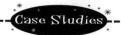

Scripture Passages

Psalm 19:7-10; 119:103,105; Ezekiel 3:3; John 1:1-5,14,18; Colossians 3:16; 2 Timothy 3:16; 1 John 4:8-10

Moodiness

Soon after Jana turned 14, she seemed to become a different person. Before that, Jana was a very good student with lots of friends and a great relationship with her parents; now she is unmotivated in school and rude and disrespectful to her mom and dad. Recently, Jana lost a couple of very good friendships because she is so moody and emotional.

Discussion Questions

1. As a friend of Jana what might you say to her?

2. What are a few things Jana or her friends can do to help her overcome her moodiness?

Possible Topics

Moodiness; friendships; family; accountability

Scripture Passages

Ephesians 4:15-16; 6:1; Colossians 3:20; Hebrews 10:24-25

The Note

Tawni loved to write notes in class. She had lots of friends, and she was always giving or receiving a note from someone. Some of the notes were quite graphic, particularly those shared between Tawni and her friend Erica.

One day when Tawni got home from school, her mother was waiting for her at the kitchen table. Tawni could tell she was in trouble—her mom had "the look"—but she didn't know why. Then her mom pulled out a folded piece of paper, and Tawni could tell from the way it was folded that it was a note from her purse. She knew it was the one that Tawni and Erica had written back and forth to each other with some very explicit and vulgar wording.

As her mother confronted her with the contents of the note, Tawni became very defensive and angry that her mom had searched her purse.

Discussion Questions

1. Was Tawni's mom right in looking through Tawni's purse?

2. Where was Tawni at fault?

3. What would have been the best way for Tawni's mom to handle the situation?

4. What advice might you give to Tawni?

5. What advice might you give to Tawni's mother?

Possible Topics

Friendships; sexuality; language; parents; handling conflict

Scripture Passages

1 Corinthians 6:18-20; Ephesians 4:29-30; 1 Thessalonians 4:3-8

Only One Time

Sarah was like any other Christian girl, or so it was thought. She had been going to church since she was a baby and had been involved in everything. She had been in children's choir and youth choir. She went on mission trips and was on the student leadership team. Then came her senior year of high school.

Sarah had always liked guys who were a bit on the wild side. Yet she had always persuaded them to come to church with her. She even seemed to be a positive influence on them. Then came Ryan. Ryan was, well, *hot*. He was one of the most popular guys in school, so when Ryan asked her out, Sarah said, "Yes." This was the beginning of the most wonderful romance of her life. They went everywhere together. Sarah got Ryan to attend church and even to go on a youth group retreat.

During spring break, Sarah, Ryan and their friends spent the week at the beach, staying in some condos. It was a typical spring break week when anything goes. In fact, Sarah tried it all: drinking, marijuana and sex. Sarah and Ryan had sex once that week. Sarah thought the experience was not as good as everyone said it was supposed to be. After a long talk on the way home, Sarah and Ryan decided not to have sex again.

A couple of months went by and Sarah and Ryan were having the time of their lives. They were getting ready for college, going on church youth trips and having romantic dates. During this time they had not had sex again. But one day, Sarah realized that she had missed her last two periods. She went to the store and bought a pregnancy test kit, and it turned out that she was pregnant. She couldn't believe it! She had only had sex one time. Sarah thought, *Why did this have to happen to me?*

Discussion Questions

1. What might Sarah be feeling? What are her choices?

2. What might Ryan feel when she tells him? What are Ryan's choices?

3. What are the pros and cons if they get married?

4. When and how should they tell their parents?

5. How should the Christians in their lives respond to their situation?

6. How does God feel about this pregnancy? Why does He allow things like this to happen?

Possible Topics

Dating; sexuality; purity; experimenting; parties; spring break; abortion; adoption

Scripture Passages

Galatians 6:1-8; James 1:12-18; 4:7-12; 1 John 1:9-10

A Pinocchio Sort of Lie

Becky thought Greg was the best looking, funniest guy she had ever met. She had not had many dates, but she was hoping for one with Greg. Becky's mom, on the other hand, had told her that she thought Greg was not the right kind of boy to date. He was not a Christian, and Becky had said she was only going to date Christian boys. Yet Becky had convinced herself that since Greg came to church sometimes, this was good enough.

Then Greg asked Becky to meet him at a nearby park. It wasn't a real date, but it was close enough. It sounded fun and exciting to Becky, but she knew she had to do it without her mom knowing. That night, she went to spend the night at a friend's house, or so she told her mom.

Becky felt awkward making her friend lie to cover for her, so she told her friend she needed to run to the store for something and then went to the park to meet Greg. She had a fun time and got back to the friend's house within a couple of hours. Everything seemed under control.

> **Optional Activity:** Have students form small groups and discuss what might have happened if Becky continued to lie.

Discussion Questions

1. When did the lying begin? How would you define a lie?

2. Why do you think it made Becky feel awkward to ask her friend to lie when she was already lying?

3. How do you think Becky felt while she was telling the lies? How do you think it made others feel when and if they found out they were lied to?

4. How does a "small" lie grow into a big problem?

5. Has this ever happened to you? How did it make you feel? How did it affect your relationship with the people involved?

6. How could Becky have stopped this thing? How could she have dealt with it honestly?

Possible Topics

Lying; relationships with parents; relationships with friends; relationship with God; trust

Scripture Passages

Proverbs 6:16-17; 26:18-19,28; James 3:5-12

Prom Night Sleepover

Prom night was just two days away. For some weeks Stacey had been pleading with her parents to allow her to attend a coed sleepover after the prom, but it seemed she was making little progress in her favor. She had tried every argument she could think of and then some.

"But Mom, everybody is going to sleep over at Ricky's house after the homecoming dance."

"Ricky's mom and dad will chaperone."

"It's mostly the church youth-group kids who will be there."

"We won't be drinking or having sex."

"Don't you trust me?"

"Everyone else's parents are letting them sleep over."

"You and Dad are so old-fashioned."

Discussion Questions

1. What do you think about Stacey's dilemma?

2. Were Stacey's parents right in saying she couldn't go to the sleepover?

3. What advice would you give to Stacey?

4. What advice would you give to Stacey's parents?

Possible Topics

Parents; handling conflict; peer pressure; decision-making; communication

Scripture Passages

Proverbs 15:1; 25:11; Ephesians 6:1; Colossians 3:20

Ron's Betrayal

Ron is a friend of yours who has grown up with you. You have been close friends and have hung out with each other for years. You have plans to go with Ron next Friday to a youth group event called Mystery Night. The mystery is that the leaders haven't told you or anyone else in the youth group where you are going or what you are going to do.

On Friday afternoon Ron calls you to say that he's not feeling well and that you'll have to go by yourself. He says that he is sorry and he'll see you on Sunday, hopefully.

You go to Mystery Night by yourself. It's not too bad, though, because you have lots of other friends in the youth group who are all there. After going bowling, you all end up at a local pizza place. You and some of your other friends sit down at a table. You look across the room and see Ron sitting with some other friends from school, and they look like they are all having a great time. He looks like he's feeling fine. He sees you and looks very surprised. He is *so* busted!

Discussion Questions

1. If this happened to you, how would you react to Ron's deception?

2. How might this incident change your relationship with Ron?

3. Now change roles: If you were Ron, what would you do?

4. What would Jesus want you to do in this situation?

Possible Topics

Responding to someone who has wronged you; forgiving others; handling broken trust; judging others

Scripture Passages

Matthew 6:14-15; 7:1-5; 18:15,21-22; Romans 2:1-3; Colossians 3:13-14

Sexually Transmitted Diseases

Kristen considered herself a really good kid. She didn't smoke or drink, and she almost lived at the church where she enjoyed the activities. When a really cute guy from her history class asked her to go to the homecoming dance, she was absolutely elated. Even though Kristen had already decided that she would not date non-Christians, she reasoned with herself, thinking *It's only one dance and besides, what can it hurt? Jaime is really nice; in fact, he's nicer than some of the guys in my youth group!*

At the dance, Jaime was a true gentleman. Afterward, he began to call Kristen and they talked every day on the phone for hours. Soon they were spending every moment they could together. Kristen had a feeling that this relationship was not right, but she was having so much fun and enjoying the attention that she put those feelings out of her mind.

As their relationship became serious, Kristen listened less to her conscience and more to her emotions. After many months of going out with Jaime, Kristen developed some sores. When she went to the doctor, he gave her a complete physical exam. Kristen couldn't believe what her doctor was telling her—she stared in disbelief as she learned that she had been infected with an incurable disease called herpes.

Discussion Questions

1. What is herpes?

2. How can you get herpes?

3. What could Kristen have done to prevent contracting herpes?

4. What advice would you have given Kristen early in her relationship with Jaime?

5. What advice would you give her now that she has herpes?

Possible Topics

Sexuality; purity; sexually transmitted diseases; dating; relationships

Scripture Passages

Proverbs 6:28; 1 Corinthians 6:18-20; 1 Thessalonians 4:3-8

A Shameful Date

Ashley was popular in school, active in church and growing as a Christian. At church camp she met Jason and fell madly in love with him. Jason was a year older than Ashley and was on his high school basketball team.

They started going out nearly every weekend. Ashley loved everything about Jason: he was cute, athletic, exciting and smart, had a great personality and was *so* much fun. But from the beginning, Ashley felt torn. Jason wasn't a bad guy, but he didn't share some of Ashley's values: he struggled with his faith, and he liked to party. He would invite Ashley to attend his basketball games and afterwards they would go to parties where beer flowed freely. Jason would sometimes join in the drinking, but she never actually saw him get drunk like the others. He seemed to drink just to be sociable, and he always treated her well—never teasing her or allowing others to tease her about not drinking. And yet, she always felt uncomfortable about the things that went on at these parties.

Jason was having an awesome year in basketball: his high school team was undefeated and made it to the finals. Ashley got special permission from her parents to attend the final game, even though it was in another city 20 miles away. She cheered as loud as the rest of the fans when the team won 103-101 in overtime. Everyone went to a pizza place to celebrate, but then most of Jason's friends ended up at a motel. Ashley didn't want to go; but Jason insisted, "Just for a little while, please!"

Jason was stoked about his part in the championship win and seemed to be drinking more than usual, getting drunker by the moment. Ashley refused the beer that was offered to her, but she did drink a couple of sodas that Jason handed her. After a while she began to feel kind of weird and dizzy, and she decided to go outside. The next thing she knew she was waking up in the back of her car in the motel parking lot. As she tried to sort things out, she vaguely remembered Jason taking her out to her car and forcing himself on her. She was devastated and ashamed of herself for being in this situation. She didn't know what to do.

Discussion Questions

1. What should Ashley do?

2. Many women in this situation feel that they are at fault. In the case of date rape, who's at fault and why?

3. What, if anything, can women do to protect themselves from date rape?

4. Imagine that you are Ashley's friend (or youth pastor) and she calls you for help. What would you do? What advice would you give her?

Possible Topics
Date rape; substance abuse; dating relationships

Scripture Passages
2 Corinthians 6:14; Ephesians 5:11,15,18; 1 Thessalonians 4:3-8

Suicide

"I hate my family, I hate my church, I hate life. I want to die—I've even thought about ways I would kill myself." When Mrs. Centeno, Sara's third-period teacher, intercepted Sara's note to Mark, she knew she had to report this potential suicide to the authorities.

Mrs. Centeno asked Sara to stay after class. When they were alone, Sara begged her teacher not to tell her parents about the note, saying that she really didn't mean it. Concerned, Mrs. Centeno wanted Sara to get the help she needed.

Discussion Questions

1. If you were the teacher, what would you do?

2. If you were Mark, what would you do?

3. How could Psalm 139 offer hope to Sara?

Possible Topics
Suicide; death; friendship; family

Scripture Passages
Nehemiah 9:6; Psalm 139; 1 Peter 5:7

Terrorism

September 11, 2001 is a day that will never be forgotten. Carolyn and Jason were standing outside the high school library at their school in Montclair, New Jersey, just across the water from New York City. Carolyn looked up and actually watched the first plane fly into the first of the World Trade Center towers. As they watched in disbelief, another plane dove into the second tower. Shocked, Jason and Carolyn stood with many of their classmates watching in horror as both buildings tumbled to the ground.

Carolyn went into shock. Even as the months pass, pushing the horrible events further into the past, she is still unable to bounce back. In a state of deep depression, Carolyn is afraid to be alone in her house; she doesn't like to look at the New York City skyline—once her favorite view in the world; she has trouble sleeping; and even her faith in God has been shaken.

Jason, on the other hand, lost a cousin on the 93rd story of the South Tower to the cowardly act of terrorism. Like Carolyn, the rest of the nation and much of the world, Jason was very saddened by what had happened. Unlike Carolyn, however, Jason's sadness was added to by his having lost a loved one in the tower. Yet he seems to be stronger in his faith and more intense about building special family memories—and he appears much more resilient than Carolyn.

Both Carolyn and Jason are involved in the same youth group.

Discussion Questions

1. What advice would you have for Jason?

2. What advice would you have for Carolyn?

3. If Carolyn came to you and asked, "Why would God allow something like this to happen?" what might you say to her?

4. Read Isaiah 45:6-7; Lamentations 3:37-38 and Romans 8:28. How do you reconcile what happened on 9-11 and what God says in these passages?

5. What does it mean that "God is in control" or that He is "sovereign"?

Possible Topics

God's sovereignty; suffering; evil; terrorism; fear; faith

Scripture Passages

Isaiah 45:6-7; Lamentations 3:37-38, Romans 8:28

Verbal and Physical Abuse

Lauren and her mom argued more than most mothers and daughters. Family members told them over and over again that the reason they fought was because they were more alike than they would admit. Neither of them knew how to handle conflict. When Lauren was angry with her mom, she would scream "I hate you!" and call her mom terrible names.

The problem continued to escalate, and lately Lauren's mom began to lose her temper at Lauren's outbursts and she responded by slapping Lauren in the face. The times of Lauren's and her mom's losing control of themselves were getting more and more out of hand.

Lauren was afraid that one day her mother would hurt her really bad. After her mother hit her, she would usually come back when things calmed down and apologize for losing control. Lauren knew she shouldn't talk back to her mom, but she also knew that her mom was not right in hitting her.

Discussion Questions

1. What are the issues in this case study?

2. What does this family need to do?

3. Where is the mom at fault? Where is Lauren at fault?

4. If Lauren came to you, what advice would you give her?

Possible Topics

Physical abuse; handling conflict; anger; family

Scripture Passages

Proverbs 15:1; Zephaniah 3:17; 1 Peter 5:7

Violence at School

Katie was very aware that every school has its share of potentially dangerous kids. In fact, she had always been afraid that the violence in schools she had heard so much about would one day happen at her school. One day Katie heard a rumor about a boy she knew by sight but had never talked to. The rumor was that he was talking about imitating the shootings carried out at Columbine High School in 1999.

Katie talked with her friends about telling someone in the school office, but everyone said it would be a waste of time. Besides, they reasoned, if it were true and the boy found out who told on him, he might want revenge. It seemed that everyone she talked to either didn't take the threat seriously or was afraid to get involved. Katie wanted to do something about the potential problem but didn't know what to do.

Discussion Questions

1. If you were Katie, what would you do?

2. Do you have any of these same fears about someone at your school?

3. What do you think are some of the reasons students turn to violence at school?

4. What can be done to stop it, if anything?

Possible Topics
School violence; peer pressure; decision making; responsibility

Scripture Passages
Ezekiel 33:1-9; James 4:17

Discussion Starters

The Barf Bag

> **Note:** This discussion starter works best with middle school/junior high students.

Materials Needed

Airplane barf (motion sickness) bags for everyone. If you can't get those, purchase brown lunch bags.

Share the following story:

> A woman traveled by plane to a conference. Although the woman was prone to airsickness, this was a short flight and she thought that she would not get sick. Unfortunately, she became very nauseous. She found a barf bag in the pocket of the seat in front of her, but she chose not to use it. She waited patiently. As the plane arrived at the airport gate, she made a mad dash to be the first off the plane. She had to get to a restroom as quickly as possible and then make her connecting flight. As it turned out, the woman had waited too long and while walking up the ramp, she vomited on herself and the man who was walking in front of her, ruining his suit. Flight attendants helped them clean up. The woman also missed her connecting flight. All this because she did not use the bag that was provided for her.

Discuss: What's the point? The point is this: God has given us many tools to use when we have a crisis or when life is too busy, but we do not use them. Tools such as prayer, His Word, Christian friends and mentors are always available to help us. God provided for our needs before we even knew we had them. Yet, like the woman in the story, pride, busyness, thinking we have everything under control and not knowing exactly how to use the tools God gives us can cause us to miss out and, very often, end up in even worse situations.

How about you? Do you know about the tools that God gives us for those times of crisis? Will you use them?

Discussion Questions

1. What is a situation you've been in, in which you thought you had everything under control, but it turned out that you did not?

2. How would you handle the situation differently now?

3. When have you ignored God's tools and resources that could have helped you in a difficult situation?

4. Next time you face a difficult situation, what can you do to remind yourself of God's tools that can help you?

Possible Topics

Prayer; Bible study; fellowship with believers

Scripture Passages

Romans 15:4; 2 Timothy 3:16-17; 2 Peter 1:3-9

I Never

Preparation

You will need a chair for each person in the group.

To play this game, the group makes a circle with their chairs and sits down. Place an "It" chair in the middle of the circle. An adult leader should sit in the It chair to begin the game. Explain the game: **There are two basic rules. Everyone must agree to these rules to make it fun.**

1. **Everyone must tell the truth.**
2. **Everyone must move at least two seats from his or her present seat when it is his or her turn to move.**

The person who is It calls out something that he or she has never done. (Examples: "I've never been to Europe" or "I've never worn a dress" or "I've never had a pet dog.") **Those who have done whatever It says must jump up and run to find a new seat. In the meantime, the person who is It tries to find a new seat. The person who is left standing is the new It. The game continues in this manner.** It will be rowdy and noisy but an opportunity to get to know a little about one another. Play for a few minutes and then have everyone sit down as you discuss the questions. **Hint:** Never play a game so long that students start to get bored. Stop short of that point, leaving them anxious for more!

Discussion Questions

1. What is something everyone has done? (Some of the responses might be breathing, eating, sleeping, going to school, etc.—but eventually lead the discussion to sin.) Read Romans 3:23 and talk about how all have sinned and fallen short of the glory of God.

3. What is something that God has never done? (Sinned.)

4. Read Hebrews 4:15 and 1 Peter 2:22. How is Jesus different from us?

5. What is something God has never stopped doing? (Again, there can be several answers, so let them talk.)

Possible Topics

We are all sinners; God has never stopped loving us; accepting God's plan of salvation

Scripture Passages

John 3:16; Romans 3:23; 5:8; 6:23; 1 John 4:8-10

I Would Live for the Lord

If I had one year to live, I would love others more.
I would choose to laugh and shed fewer tears.
I would smile at everyone that passed me by.
And I would choose not to worry.

I would live for the Lord.

If I had one year to live, I would give more hugs.
I would claim the peace that my Lord offers.
I would do cartwheels and not care who was looking.
And I would choose not to criticize.

I would live for the Lord.

If I had one year to live, I would tell those I care about just how much
    I do care.
I would choose to share memories and make some more.
I would give all—all I had.
And I would choose to not find importance in things.

I would live for the Lord.

If I had one year to live, I would practice my guitar.
I would choose to give the Lord more than I ever thought I could.
I would share my faith and not be afraid.
And I would choose to not be selfish.

I would live for the Lord.

If I had one year to live I would smell the beautiful flowers.
I would run through wild fields and climb really big trees.
I would seek solitude in the weeping willow and in my Lord.

And I wouldn't be so ignorant of the beauty of life.

I would live for the Lord.

If I had one year to live, I would practice obedience.
I would choose to follow Him instead of running ahead.
I would listen and fall in love with Him over and over.
And I would desire to be used to bring glory to His name.

I would live for the Lord.

Discussion Questions

1. If you had one year to live, what would you want to do?

2. If you could do one thing better, what would you do?

3. How might thinking that you only had one year to live change your perspectives about your life?

4. How do you want to be remembered when you die?

5. How can you live more focused on what is really important? What things, attitudes or activities would you want to change as a result of this discussion?

Possible Topics

Abundant life; the Christian life; making the most of every opportunity; setting right priorities

Scripture Passages

Psalm 23:5-6; John 10:10; 1 Corinthians 9:24-25; Ephesians 5:15-17; Philippians 3:12-14; Hebrews 12:1-3

The Parable of the Good Samaritan— Luke 10:25-37

Assign the following roles and instruct the actors to perform the actions as a leader reads the story. Be sure to read the story slowly enough to allow the actors to ham it up!

The Samaritan

A donkey

The victim

The bed (two people)

Two robbers

A rock

A priest

Innkeeper

A Levite

One day, a Bible expert stood up to question Jesus in order to test him.

"Teacher, what do I need to do to go to heaven?"

Jesus answered the man with his own question, "What does the Bible say?"

The man said back, "It tells us to love God as hard and as much as we can; and love our neighbors as much as we love ourselves."

Jesus said, "Good answer! Do those two things, and you'll really be living!"

But the man tried to find a way out because he really didn't want to love others, so he asked Jesus, "Who exactly is my neighbor?" So Jesus told him this story:

One day a man was walking from Jerusalem to Jericho. The journey was long, and he started panting like a dog because it was so hot outside. He got so tired that he sat down on a rock. While he was resting, robbers were lurking nearby. They spotted the man sitting on the rock. They pointed at him. They sneered at him.

One of the robbers said, "Let's jump him."

The other robber said, "Let me think about it for awhile. Hmm. Hmm."

Finally he said, "Yeah! Let's jump him, steal all of his money and beat the snot out of him too!"

So the robbers crept up behind the man sitting on the rock. They knocked the man off of the rock. They attacked him. They stole all of his stuff. They even picked up the big rock and threw it on the man. They left him for dead.

The man was terribly beat up. He tried to get up, but the big rock was on him and it was too heavy. The man gasped and fainted. When he regained consciousness, he managed to squeeze out from under the rock. He tried to get up. He got to his feet. But he was just too weak, so he fell down. Then he fainted again.

Luckily a priest was walking down the same road. When he saw the man lying unconscious, he stopped. Standing over the man, he yelled out, "Why don't these homeless people get jobs like everyone else?"

He folded his arms. He threw back his head in disgust. Then he carefully walked over to the other side of the road, passing by the wounded man.

A little bit later, another religious man, a Levite, showed up. When he came to the wounded man, he found him awake but groaning because he was in pain. The man groaned. And he groaned. And he groaned some more. The Levite got down on his knees beside the hurt man, who was still groaning. He picked up the wounded man's head, cradling it in his hands, and said, "Quit groaning, you're making a scene!"

The hurting man cried, "Please help me."

The Levite replied, "I'm sorry, I can't. I've got a 2:30 appointment in Jericho to give some money to the poor."

With that the Levite dropped the man's head to the ground. He got up. He started walking away. He stopped all of a sudden and turned around to the man and said: "Oh, I almost forgot to tell you: God loves you and so do I." With that he turned and walked away.

A while later, a Samaritan traveling the road on his donkey came up to the wounded man, who had lost consciousness again. He got off his donkey and kneeled down beside the man. His heart went out to the man. He began weeping over the man. He picked the man up and held him in his arms, weeping and weeping. The man woke up while he was in the Samaritan's arms; and being confused from his head injury cried out, "Mommy!" He fainted again. The Samaritan lifted the man onto his donkey and led him to a nearby inn where he laid him on the bed in his room. The bed had one of those old Magic Fingers machines that make beds shake. The Samaritan put a quarter in and the bed really shook. It shook and shook! The wounded man really liked it and he yelled, "Yippee!" Then he fainted again.

The next morning the Samaritan went to the innkeeper and said, "Hey pal, here's my American Express. Take good care of my friend in the room. Whatever he needs, give it to him and charge it to my card."

Jesus then asked the Bible expert, "What do you think? Which of the three acted like a neighbor to the man attacked by the robbers?"

The man replied, "Obviously it was the one who treated him kindly."

Jesus said, "Go and love your neighbors in the same way."

Discussion Questions

1. How can you influence someone else's life by the way you love and serve them?

2. What makes it difficult for you to demonstrate love by serving others?

3. How is it possible to love people we don't even like?

4. What are some specific ways in which you can demonstrate love to people in your life during the next week?

Possible Topics

Loving others; kindness; brotherly love; servanthood; helping the needy

Scripture Passages

Luke 6:27-36; 10:25-37; James 1:27; 2:14-17; 1 John 3:18

A Personal Jesus

Materials Needed

- ❑ Someone to play Jesus
- ❑ A long robe
- ❑ Sandals
- ❑ A walking stick
- ❑ Slips of paper or index cards
- ❑ Pens or pencils

Preparation

Arrange for someone (preferably with long hair) to come to the youth-group meeting as the person of Christ. Advertise the meeting a couple of weeks ahead of time, saying that a special guest will be attending, but give no clues. Have the person who is pretending to be Jesus wear casual clothes as he comes to the meeting, but then change into the robe and sandals after the opening game.

Begin the meeting with an outdoor game in which everyone plays. Have "Jesus" join in the fun with the students.

Next, retire to the meeting room, but have the Jesus character slip off to another room to change into the robe and sandals and get the walking stick. While he is changing, give students slips of paper and pens or pencils and instruct them to write questions that they'd like to ask Jesus. Collect the papers, and then explain: **We promised that we would have a special guest today, and here he is—Jesus!** After a moment of loud applause, explain that "Jesus" will answer some of the questions that they have written out. (**Note:** This might be even more effective if you have students write these out the week before so that the Jesus character has had some time to prepare. As you probably know, students can ask some tough questions!) After he has answered some questions, ask the students which Jesus they find it easier to relate to: the one who participated in the games or one that looks like something out of an Easter pageant?

Finish by helping students see that Jesus is alive and present with them today. He's not just a historical figure who lived and died 2,000 years ago. He can handle today's issues and problems.

Discussion Questions

Use the questions that students wrote down as discussion questions. However, the big question of the lesson is which Jesus the students find it easier to relate to and why.

Possible Topics

Who is Jesus? Is Jesus relevant for today? Having a personal relationship with Jesus; seeing Jesus as a historical figure versus Jesus who is alive today

Scripture Passages

John 1:1-14; 14:6-7; 15:14-15

The Prodigal Son— Luke 15:11-32

Read Luke 15:11-32. Ask for a volunteer to be the prodigal and role-play the following three depictions of God. You will be the character of the father/God. Instruct the volunteer to walk up to you and you will do the acting. Expand on the stories as you see fit.

A Spineless Pushover

(In an ambivalent tone, play out the story of the prodigal as he or she approaches his or her father. Look disinterested, and never face the prodigal. Look away and become distracted.)

"Oh, hi, son. How's it going? Yeah, we missed you, but we knew you needed some space. (Picks at lint on his son's clothes) **How long has it been? Oh, that long? My, well, I'm surprised. Yeah, bet you've seen a lot.** (Looks off and around) **No, no. You can tell me sometime later. Maybe next week. Oh, now, don't be sorry. No apology needed. Just go along and live your life. I can't condemn you for that. No, sir. Just goin' with the flow.**"

A Severe Vindicator

(Stand on a chair with arms crossed and angry. Shout and talk loudly as you narrate this tirade. Lean into and over the prodigal. Must be angry, but exploring passive anger might work too. Don't just yell as it will distract. Talk angrily and firmly and yell upon occasion.)

"**Oh, so there you are! Like I want to see you now. After all you put your mother and me through. The work we had to do because you wanted to see the world. And what a mess you left in your room. I can tell you there's no mess anymore. Nope, we rented your room and gave your junk to the Salvation Army. Like your things were worth anything. Don't look to me for a loan or anything else. If you're hungry, work like the rest of the help. You left me with the harvest, and I've had to milk those stupid goats myself. I can't even believe that you're here again! Don't figure that your mom's going to be glad to see you either—the way you worried that poor woman . . .**"

> **Warning:** Even students from the best homes may have an emotional reaction to this parent. It is important to debrief this activity!

Our Daddy

Turn around and spot the prodigal and then cry out "**Thank God, thank God.**" Run to the prodigal, embrace him/her. Embrace and release as you work through the dialogue. This one is best with longer and shorter pauses between the sentences.

"**Oh, how I've missed you! Praise God that you've returned! I looked for you on the road every morning, and I prayed you would come home safely as I looked for you every evening. I'm so glad you've returned. Your mother will be ecstatic! What a blessing to see you again. And it is none too soon by the look of your clothes. I've got just the robe for you. Have you lost weight? Oh, the party I'm going to throw for you. We'll put some meat on those bones.**"

Discussion Questions

1. Which God do you prefer to have a relationship with?

2. Why is the Daddy God so attractive?

3. How does it feel to know that God loves and accepts us as we are and is committed to make us even better?

4. What reactions did you feel about the spineless and angry versions of God?

Possible Topics

Restoration; sin and forgiveness; What is God like?

Scripture Passages

Luke 15:11-32; John 3:16-17; Galatians 4:6-7; 1 John 3:1

Walking on Water— Matthew 14:22-33

Select seven people to be a part of a role-play. Assign one person to be Jesus, one person to be Peter and the other five people to be the disciples. Have the disciples take their places in the imaginary boat. As you read Matthew 14:22-33, pause to allow actors to act out their parts. Encourage them to be creative and expressive.

After the scene is completed, walk students back through the scene, focusing on the dialogue between Jesus and Peter. Remind students that as long as Peter kept his eyes focused on Jesus, he stayed on top of the water; as soon as he turned his attention to his circumstances, he began to sink.

Discussion Questions

1. What situation in your life seems as impossible as walking on water?

2. If you were absolutely convinced that Jesus would enable you to make it through this situation, what would you do to face it head-on?

3. What makes it difficult to keep your eyes focused on Jesus?

4. What can you do to stay focused on Jesus?

Possible Topics

Keeping focused on Jesus; facing challenges; seeing the seemingly impossible as possible; the dangers of self-reliance

Scripture Passages

Proverbs 14:12; Matthew 14:22-33; John 15:4-8

Topical Index

Scripture Reference Index
Old Testament

Page numbers in **boldface** type indicate Key Verses.

New Testament

Page numbers in **boldface** type indicate Key Verses.

Page numbers in **boldface** type indicate Key Verses.

Page numbers in **boldface** type indicate Key Verses.